itive therapy • ... evelop the

on't stress about money • understand the

take control • ask uplifting questions •

grateful • change your breathing • develop

e omega-3 • set clear goals • release your

on your self-image • change focus • be an

augh • seek internal goals • simplify your

-actualizer • get busy • smile • get some

e by the confucian theory • balance alone

alcohol consumption • take L-tyrosine •

meet new people • turn off the TV • dress

up • kiss someone • focus on happiness

better than chocolate

BETTER THAN
Chocolate

50 Proven Ways
to Feel Happier

siimon reynolds

illustrations by jenny kostecki

TEN SPEED PRESS
Berkeley | Toronto

↑☺
Ten Speed Press
P.O. Box 7123
Berkeley, California 94707
www.tenspeed.com

Distributed in Canada by Ten Speed Press Canada.

Cover and interior design by Betsy Stromberg

First published by the Penguin Group (Australia) in 2004.

Library of Congress Cataloging-in-Publication Data
Reynolds, Siimon.
  Better than chocolate : 50 proven ways to feel happier / Siimon Reynolds ;
illustrations by Jenny Kostecki.
      p. cm.
  Includes bibliographical references.
  ISBN 1-58008-657-8
  1. Happiness. I. Title.
  BJ1481.R495 2005
  158.1—dc22
                            2004026820

First printing, 2005

Printed in China
1 2 3 4 5 6 7 8 9 10 — 09 08 07 06 05

To Kath,
source of so much happiness.

contents

introduction

What could possibly be better than chocolate?
How about good health, self-acceptance, loving relationships, freedom from fear and guilt, and a clear
sense of purpose in life? **Happiness is not an
accident.** There are numerous simple techniques
anyone can use to live a more joyful life. The only
trouble is, few people know about them or seek them out.

The field of **Positive Psychology,** or the study of how
to be happy, is one of the newest areas of science. News
of its discoveries has yet to reach many people. In this
small guide, I've attempted to summarize a range of
major ancient and contemporary theories on happiness.
I have deliberately kept them brief and simple so that
you may grasp the keys to increasing your bliss
without having to wade through mountains of scientific
research. These techniques have all been tested, many

under rigorous clinical conditions, and they've been **proven not just effective but life-changing.**

Though it may not satisfy your immediate sweet tooth, *Better Than Chocolate* should put a smile on your face and some joy in your heart. **More important, I hope you'll try to make these happiness-inducing techniques and principles a part of your life.** After all, there is surely nothing more important in our lives than our happiness.

HAPPY READING.

things that make me HAPPY...

my dog

falling leaves

triple decker ice cream cones

rainbows

colored socks

if you're feeling listless, make a list

MAKE A
happiness list

When I first heard of this technique I was struck by its simplicity. High-performance expert Fred Grosse recommends his students write a list of all the activities they love doing. It could be anything from walking on a beach at sunset to having a long soak in the bath.

Make such a list for yourself. Then, at the beginning of each week, schedule at least one of these activities in your diary every day. Allocate a specific time for it to ensure you'll make it happen. With this simple system, your life soon becomes filled with many more enjoyable, happy moments. Just as important, this technique forces you to be more conscious of your happiness and to make it a top priority.

Daily exercise can have a huge impact on how positive we feel. There are several reasons why. First, giving our body a regular workout helps reduce tension and stress. Second, studies have shown that exercise changes our body's biochemistry. During exercise we produce natural opiates, known as endorphins, that make us feel happier—hence the famous "runner's high."

Finally, regular exercise reduces fat, improves muscle tone, clears the skin, and makes us feel strong. These changes often lead to a significant increase in self-esteem, a mental state closely linked with happiness.

TRY cognitive therapy

In the last twenty years, mainstream psychology has taken an enormous leap forward. Where Freud and Jung once claimed that emotions affect our thinking, today's cognitive therapists emphasize that thinking also alters our moods. **To feel happier, they say, we must direct our thinking.**

When you next feel down, try this simple but powerful cognitive therapy technique:

1. Write down what you are thinking.

2. Question this on paper—is the thought helpful and realistic?

3. Write down a more positive way of looking at your situation.

Try it now. You'll be surprised at how this elementary cognitive process can work wonders.

GET IN flow

Flow theory is one of the most important breakthroughs of the last twenty years. Mihaly Csikszentmihalyi, its pioneer, suggests that **enjoyment consists of four components:**

1. We are doing an activity that is challenging;
2. it is clear how we are progressing (the rules are simple);
3. it takes all our concentration;
4. but we are making progress and feel in control.

We tend to experience flow when we practice a discipline such as an art or a sport or a religion. (Activities such as watching TV are not usually flowful because they lack a sense of achievement.) The more flow activities we incorporate into our lives, the happier we feel. **What five activities create flow for you, and how could you do more of them each week?**

high self-esteem

optimism

control over one's life

extroversion

happy individuals share four characteristics

DEVELOP THE four magic PERSONALITY TRAITS

According to the research of David Myers (a leading Positive Psychology therapist), people who are happier than average tend to exhibit four characteristics:

1. **high self-esteem**
2. a feeling of control over life
3. **optimism**
4. extroversion (surprising but true)

Our happiness will increase as we cultivate these personality traits. **Take a few minutes now to write down some ways you could incorporate these four traits in your own character.**

peace

peace

meditation clears your mind

meditate

Twenty years of research by Dr. Herbert Benson of Harvard Medical School shows that people who meditate regularly are usually happier than those who don't. Not sure how to meditate? He suggests this straightforward technique:

1. Choose simple, positive word, such as **"calm," "love," "one," or "peace."**

2. Repeat that word to yourself for ten to twenty minutes. You can either say the word aloud or just in your head every second or two.

3. Try to clear away everyday thoughts that come up and steer your focus back toward your repetition.

It's that easy—and that hard!

if you focus on money
happiness goes down

DON'T STRESS ABOUT money

In today's society, there is an ever-increasing array of stuff we are tempted to buy—new furniture, the latest electronics, this season's must-have dress, that hot new car . . . the list goes on. **But it's all a trap.** Growing scientific research shows that an obsession with material gain actually makes us less happy. Positive Psychology expert Martin Seligman has shown that those who focus purely on making more money are less happy than the average person.

What's more, it has been proven that once someone's income rises above the basic poverty line, there is little difference in happiness between them and the rich. Studies indicate that the availability of material possessions is nine times less vital to happiness than personal assets like friends and family. **Clearly, the old adage is true: you can't buy happiness.**

fewer desires leads to less suffering

UNDERSTAND THE
buddhist theory

Classical Buddhist theory centers on desire. Buddhists believe that our desires and attachments to the world are the cause of much of our frustration and misery. **Reducing these desires and attachments is thus a surer path to happiness.** There are two simple ways to minimize desire:

1. **Achieve what we desire.**
2. **Reduce our desires.**

Buddhists suggest that the first is extremely difficult and that the second offers a quicker road to bliss. Of course, for the average person, it doesn't make sense to have no desires at all. Where would the fun be in life? But ask yourself, "Would I be happier if I reduced the number of things I want?" **The answer may surprise you.**

balancing sugar levels sweetens your mood

TRY A low-insulin DIET

Building on the work of the controversial Robert Atkins, of the Atkins Diet fame, Barry Sears has shown that the typical Western diet—high in sugars and grains—plays havoc with our hormone balances, and therefore our emotions. As blood-sugar levels vary greatly with every meal, we experience regular mood swings.

Sears's solution, known as the Zone Diet, is to blend meat or fish with vegetables (excluding potato, pumpkin, and other simple root vegetables) and to **balance sugar levels with a piece of fruit every four hours.** This diet not only stabilizes our moods, it helps many to lose weight. Many Zone Dieters also report they are **more mentally focused and experience a significant increase in energy levels.**

happiness is linked to perceived control

take control

A common characteristic of happy people is that they feel they have control over their lives. **If you are unhappy, review your life to see where you feel things are out of control, then take action.** Too often, when we find ourselves in a difficult position, we withdraw and lick our wounds. That's okay for a while, but doing something to solve the problem usually does more good.

Write a list of all the areas in your life in which you feel you don't have control. **Now write down three things you could do to improve each situation.** Perhaps you need to tell someone how you really feel. Maybe you need to change direction or let something (or someone) go. Taking action can be hard, but if the result increases your sense of control over your life, you are likely to feel much happier for it.

why not

how?

why?

Because why?

questions can change the direction of your thinking

ASK uplifting QUESTIONS

The mind can easily be guided toward thinking happy thoughts with the use of simple questions. Regularly asking ourselves the following questions can have a noted effect on our life satisfaction:

1. **What am I happy about in my life?**
2. What is going well?
3. **What am I excited about?**
4. What can I look forward to?

For best results, ask yourself these questions each morning and at the end of the day. Be sure to take a few minutes to dwell on the pleasant and inspiring answers.

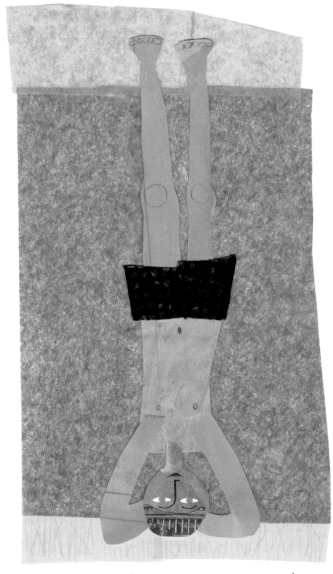

self-discipline leads to stability and contentment

DEVELOP discipline

According to the spiritualist Shaykh Fadhlalla Haeri, one of the essential factors in a person's happiness is their level of self-discipline. **Regular overindulgence in food, alcohol, sex, and even thinking can tax and weaken our body, mind, and soul.**

Practicing self-discipline in these areas strengthens our mind and self-image, as we begin to see ourselves as master of our body, rather than its slave. **Restraint leads to stability, stability to contentment.** Take a few moments to evaluate your life. In what areas do you lack self-discipline? What are three simple things you could do to tame those weaknesses?

cloudy thinking obscures happiness

CLARIFY YOUR
values

Most people are happy or miserable not because of particular events but because of how they react to them. **If we are living our life according to our values, we tend to feel happy.** If we aren't, we're less likely to feel happy. The only trouble is, most people are not clear about what they value in life.

Try this quick test. **Prioritize the following five values in order of importance in your life: health, career, family, spirituality, and social life.** Now ask yourself, "Do I live my life according to these priorities?" If not, perhaps it's time you did. Spending time choosing values to live by can be an invaluable step in simplifying your life and increasing your bliss.

feeling grateful makes it hard to be unhappy

BE grateful

This is one of the simplest happiness techniques, but also one of the most powerful. Dan Sullivan, a renowned expert in human potential, points out that it is virtually impossible to experience negative emotions when we are feeling grateful.

Because we tend to feel up or down according to what we're focusing on, a few minutes each day sitting in quiet gratitude can work wonders on our happiness level. From my own experience, I believe that constantly expressing and feeling gratitude is one of the surest ways to a lastingly happy life. **What could you be grateful for?**

oxygen intake and mood are linked

CHANGE YOUR
breathing

Every time we get angry, our breathing changes. Every time we are blissed out, it has a different pattern again. **Clearly, our moods affect our breathing.** But research has revealed it works the other way as well. If we breathe in deeply, and in a totally relaxed way, it's almost impossible to remain angry or frustrated. **Deep breathing creates a calmer, more relaxed, and happy person.**

Next time you are angry or down, try it for yourself. **Consciously alter your breathing pattern.** Breathe deeper, slower. In through the nose and out through the mouth. **Within minutes you'll find your bad mood dissolving.**

focusing on the future changes your outlook

DEVELOP
future focus

Most people have no real vision for their future. As a result, they often get caught up in day-to-day troubles. Having a future focus not only makes life more exciting, it helps make any short-term problems more bearable.

To experience a fundamentally happier life, decide where you would like to be in ten years and work toward it daily. See it clearly, believe in it. Take action to make it a reality. Take out a pen and some paper. Imagine your ideal life in a decade. Where would you live? How would you work? What would you have achieved? **It's almost impossible to feel depressed if you have a strong future focus that you work toward with hope and consistency every day.**

rivers move around obstacles

FOLLOW THE
taoist way

Taoism, along with Buddhism and Confucianism, is one of the three great philosophical schools of ancient China. The *Tao Te Ching,* the main text of Taoism, is the most translated work in the world other than the Bible.

Taoists believe that happiness can be found by following nature. For instance, water always travels around rocks, so we should try to go around problems rather than plough directly through them. When a tiger's belly is full, it stops hunting—in the same way, we should not work constantly or take more than we need. You get the picture.

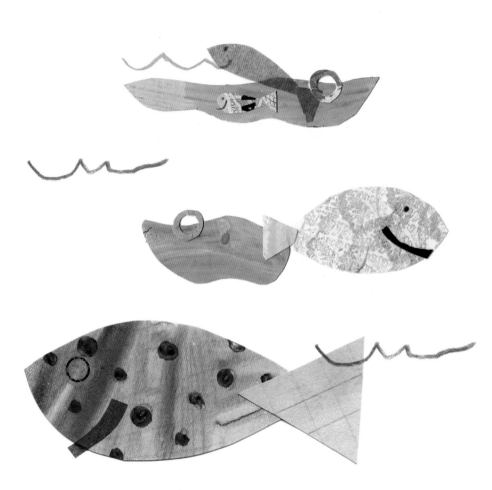

omega-3 lifts moods
(ever seen an unhappy fish?)

INCREASE
omega-3

Our diet is intricately linked to our mental state. According to Andrew Stoll of Harvard Medical School, a lack of omega-3 fats in our diet is one reason why so many people feel depressed. Stoll says study after study has shown that consuming more omega-3 helps reduce the symptoms of depression and schizophrenia, and increase happy moods.

So, how do you get more omega-3? It's easy. Just eat more deep-sea fish like salmon or tuna. Or pick up some omega-3 supplements from your pharmacist or health-food store.

spirituality

family

career

social life

education

health

exciting goals provide direction

SET clear goals

Our brains are goal-activating mechanisms. We tell our brain what we want and it devises a system for getting there. The problem, according to achievement expert Brian Tracy, is that only around 3 percent of the population set goals. No wonder so many people feel that their life has little or no direction.

It's easily remedied though. **Grab a piece of paper right now and spend ten minutes dreaming about what you would like to achieve in the following areas: health, career, social, family, spiritual, and pleasure.** Then choose your five favorite goals and begin acting—today—to make them happen. You'll find each step you take toward your goals will increase both your self-esteem and your wellbeing.

ENERGY

stretching allows
your energy to flow

Both the Indian yoga experts and the Chinese tai chi masters agree: smooth energy flow is vital for physical and mental happiness. Our bodies contain rivers of energy, known as meridians. When these are blocked we tend to feel down in the dumps.

But we don't have to spend hours sitting in the lotus position or practicing slow, repetitive movements to improve the situation. **Spending ten minutes a day stretching your major limbs and muscles helps unblock these meridians, encouraging the body's energy (*prana* in Sanskrit or *chi* in Mandarin) to circulate freely, improving both your health and your mood.**

motion changes emotion, and vice versa

ACT happy

One of the most effective happiness-inducing techniques is simply to act like you are happy. **That's right—just pretend you're in a movie, playing the part of a happy person.** Within minutes of pretending, most people report that their bad mood begins to fall away.

According to the legendary neurolinguistic programming therapists John Grinder and Richard Bandler, the reason is connected to how body movements affect thinking patterns. **They discovered that if you move like you are happy (stop slouching, don't drop your head, and so on) you begin to think happy thoughts.** Amazing, but true. As Grindler and Bandler put it, motion creates emotion.

sound sleep calms mood swings

INCREASE
sleep

In today's society many of us simply do not get enough sleep. A regular shortage of sleep not only makes us physically tired—it also lowers mood and increases irritability, according to sleep therapist and happiness psychologist Timothy Sharp.

Ideal sleep amounts vary from person to person, but usually any amount less than six hours is detrimental to our mood and our body's repair systems. **Most people need seven to eight hours of sleep per night**. If you have trouble sleeping, try eating earlier in the evening, meditating, or taking a soothing bath before you hit the sack.

as you see yourself, you become

WORK ON YOUR
self-image

Plastic surgeon Maxwell Maltz, in his pioneering work *Psycho-Cybernetics*, showed that we usually behave in accordance with the image we have of ourselves. Over time he noticed that the most important factor in a person's happiness was not what they actually looked like, but their self-image. For example, if you view yourself as an unhappy person, your brain will make sure you experience life in accordance with that.

But Maltz showed that our self-image can be re-sculpted, little by little. **By visualizing yourself being happy for a few minutes each day** (literally watching a movie of yourself in your mind), **you can improve your levels of life satisfaction significantly.**

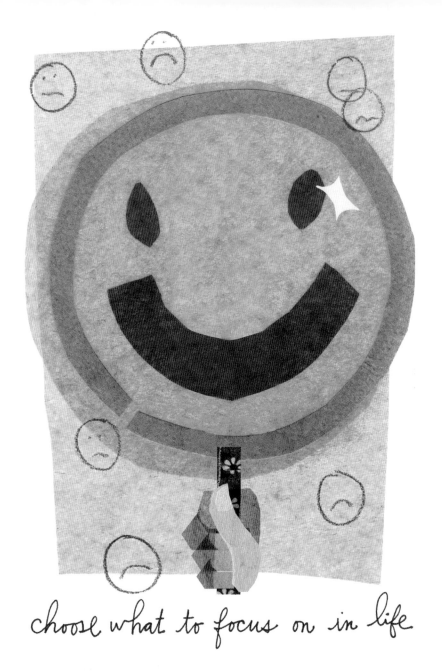

choose what to focus on in life

CHANGE
focus

Popularized by high-performance coach Anthony Robbins, the Focus Control method of happiness shows quick and powerful results. Robbins argues that we are happy or unhappy largely because of what we focus on. By consciously choosing to focus on what is going well in our life, rather than what may be going poorly, we tend to remain in a buoyant mood.

It's simple to do. **Just make a list of five things going well in your life and remind yourself of them several times throughout the day.** Within a few days, you'll find your perceptions of the quality of your life will change for the better.

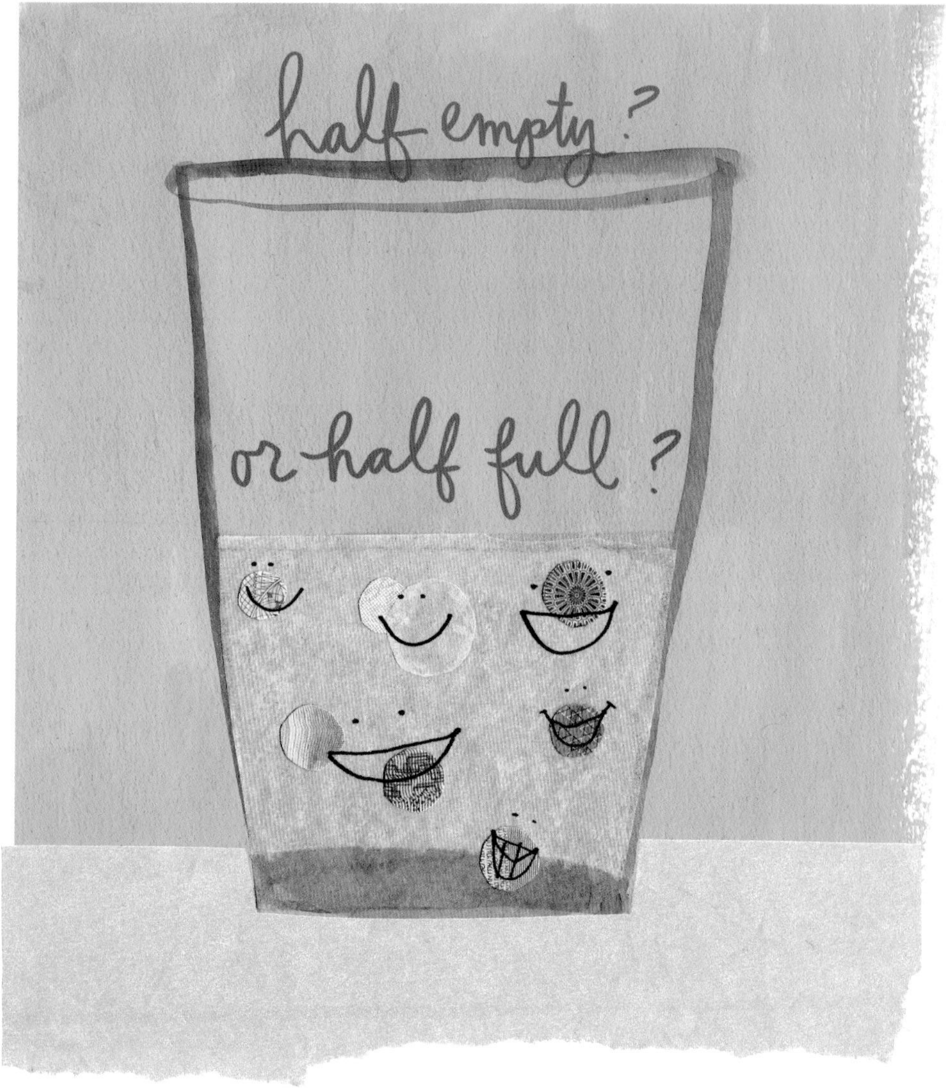

it's up to you

BE AN
optimist

Martin Seligman's pioneering work has shown that thinking optimistically is a highly effective way to increase wellbeing. Seligman has shown that optimistic people:

- are more successful at work
- experience more life enjoyment
- are healthier
- have more friends

Primarily because they see problems as temporary and don't take them personally, optimists have life enjoyment levels far higher than pessimistic people. After all, it's not the events in our lives that make us happy or sad, but our perception of those events. By choosing to look on the good side of any hardship (and there is *always* something good), and electing to believe in ourselves and our ability to conquer or recover, there really is nothing that can get us down permanently.

What problems could you think more positively about?

send love and you'll get more love back

Many people who are unhappy are too wrapped up in their own lives. The esteemed psychologist and Sufi spiritual master Javad Nurbakhsh believes unhappy people often feel better if they take the focus away from themselves and focus instead on how others are doing. **Whether it's a gift, a helping hand, or a kind word, showing another that you care is one of the quickest and most effective ways to feel good.**

Think about it. Could it be that you are a little too self-obsessed? Could over-thinking your situation be the cause of your distress? Resolve to focus on helping other people. Caring for others not only helps you forget your own problems, it can also be a hugely uplifting experience in itself. **It's no wonder that, on average, people who volunteer in their community feel twice as happy with themselves than non-volunteers.**

Namaste.

spiritual people are often healthier and happier

Those who actively participate in some form of spiritual practice are often happier than those who do not. What's more, research shows they get divorced less, keep their jobs longer, and are usually healthier than their non-spiritual counterparts.

Many psychologists believe that people's faith in a loving deity or something great than themselves also inspires them to worry less. As they look at themselves as part of a larger plan or scheme, their general life contentment increases. Interestingly, those who practice spirituality as part of a group experience more of these benefits than those who practice alone.

hoo hoo hoo

haha

hahaha

hee hee hee

laughter lifts your mood

laugh

This may seem a simplistic antidote to unhappiness, but there is plenty of evidence to support it as an effective one. A classic case study on the effects of humor on wellbeing was written by Norman Cousins in his book *Anatomy of an Illness*.

Cousins suffered from a rare degenerative disease that he cured himself using a most unusual treatment. **He watched comedies on TV for hours, read funny books, and spent loads of time laughing each day.** Within months he was completely cured. A true story. And a great reminder of the healing power of laughter, even if it is systematically arranged.

the key to happiness is inside you

You can set yourself two types of goals:

1. **internal** (quality relationships, wellbeing, personal growth, and so on)

2. **external** (money, power, fame, and so on)

Each type of goal is worthwhile, but research by Tim Kasser and Richard M. Ryan, professors of psychology, has shown that the more you develop yourself internally, the happier you will usually be. After interviewing hundreds of people and examining their life priorities, Kasser and Ryan concluded, "In sum, the pursuit of personal goals for money, fame, and attractiveness is shown to lead to a lower quality of life than the goals of relatedness, self-acceptance, and community feeling."

Take a look at your goals. Will they genuinely develop you as a person or will they merely change your outward circumstances?

juggling too much makes you unhappy

simplify YOUR LIFE

Modern life has become ridiculously busy and complex. By doing less, owning less, worrying less, and pushing ourselves less, we can often restore a sense of balance and contentment to our lives. If the complexity of your life is making you unhappy, **try these life simplifiers:**

- Throw out a third of your clothes, books, and possessions you do not absolutely need.
- Reduce your daily work hours by 10 percent.
- Schedule three nights a week when you do nothing social.
- See less of the friends or family who exhaust you.
- Spend twenty minutes a day sitting on a sofa doing nothing.

Follow these steps and you'll find that within weeks you're more organized, less tired, and considerably happier.

discover your life purpose

In his classic book *Man's Search for Meaning*, psychologist Victor Frankl showed that prisoners in Nazi concentration camps during World War II who wanted to survive *for a particular reason* often lived longer than prisoners who had no concrete goal.

Purpose or meaning in our lives is crucial.

In fact, many happiness experts believe a sense of meaning or purpose is the attribute most strongly associated with life satisfaction. Frankl even created a new type of psychology—known as Logotherapy—based around this theory.

Why are you alive? **Develop a life mission statement**— a simple paragraph that sums up your main aim in life. Post it up in your home and workplace, and work toward it daily. As you get clearer about and more committed to your life mission, your level of life satisfaction will rise.

a self-actualized
topiary artist

unlocking your inner potential leads to lasting satisfaction

BECOME A
self-actualizer

Several decades ago, Abraham Maslow became famous
in psychology circles with his theory of Self-Actualization.
In order to feel that all our needs are being met, Maslow
believed that we need to find our calling. He claimed that,
to be lastingly happy, we need the opportunity to unlock
our inner potential.

According to Maslow, self-actualizers have developed a
wide range of abilities, including:

- **self-acceptance**
- the ability to maintain loving relationships
- freedom from social pressures and conformity
- a clear sense of purpose and meaning in life

**Which of these could you work on to enhance
your life satisfaction?** What could you do to release
your inner potential and get closer to your calling?

staying busy means less time to worry

GET
busy

Over the years, I have often seen friends with little to do slipping into a state of mild depression and lethargy. My observation has been backed up by recent research in the field of Positive Psychology. Apparently the brain craves "ordered consciousness" and is happier when it has a series of challenging tasks to do.

If you are experiencing down times, create a daily to-do list each morning and get busy. When life seems gloomy, the less time you have to think (and think and think) about your situation, the happier you will often be.

simply smiling puts you in good humor

Believe it or not, there has been loads of research on smiling and the power it has to improve a person's mood. **Put simply, if you smile you are likely to feel happier.**

Researchers Rachel Kettner and Lee-Anne Hather of the University of California studied class photos from a 1961 yearbook of Mills College, a women's college in Oakland, California. Astonishingly, they found that the women who were smiling broadly and genuinely in the photos were, on average, experiencing significantly more happiness in their lives thirty years later.

Also, let's not forget that smiling *at* people in your environment tends to put *them* in a better mood, too. As the saying goes, smile and the whole world smiles with you.

sunlight

radiates

happiness

GET SOME
sunlight

Sunlight can really lift your mood. Conversely, lack of sunlight makes many people feel down. Places like Seattle and Stockholm, where there is little sunlight in the winter, report higher suicide rates.

There are two simple ways to remedy the problem. The first is to schedule daily walks in the sun (twenty minutes should suffice). The second is to live and work in a brightly lit environment. Bright fluorescent light has been shown to have a marked uplifting effect on mood. Full-spectrum lighting (arguably the healthiest artificial light) mimics natural daylight. There are many full-spectrum lighting retailers online.

not forgiving eats away at your heart

forgive

Every great religion preaches the virtues of genuine forgiveness as a path to happiness. It's easy to see why. Failing to forgive someone eats away at our heart, filling us with anger, envy, or hatred every time we think of that person—hardly a recipe for happiness.

If you are serious about being consistently happy, there is only one thing to do: call or write to the person in question and let them know you have decided to forgive them. **If you do this genuinely, you will feel a huge weight lifted off your shoulders.** If they have passed away, write them a letter anyway. Your act of forgiveness will heal and uplift you regardless.

in the best jobs work and play are intermingled

FIND satisfying work

The research is clear: if you dislike your job, you will not enjoy a happy life. Of course, there are two solutions to this dilemma. The obvious one is to change jobs. A study by Michael Argyle, Monika Henderson, and Adrian Furnham showed that **getting a new job is likely to be one of life's most positive experiences.** (We know this, and yet some of us choose to work for years in a job we hate rather than spending a little time finding a new one.)

The second solution is to change your attitude toward your job. Ask yourself, "What is good about this job? How could I make it better? How could I design my work so that I could enjoy it?" After all, as Shakespeare said, "There is nothing either good or bad, but thinking makes it so." A genuine change in attitude can often make a boring job fun again and reignite a career.

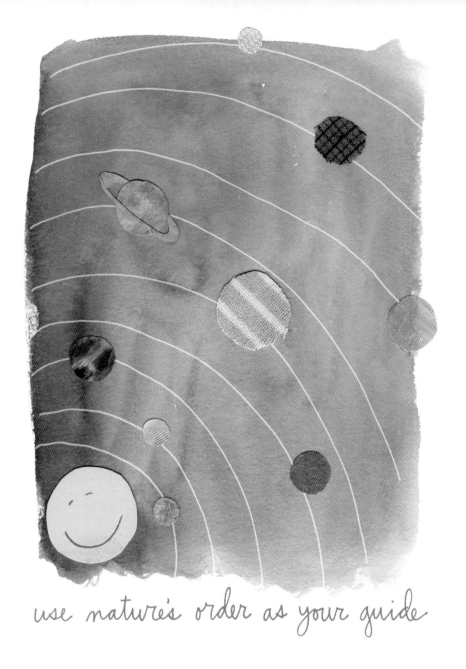

use nature's order as your guide

LIVE BY THE
confucian theory

Perhaps the most significant figure in ancient Chinese history, and certainly the most famous, Confucius developed several powerful ideas about happiness. These theories are outlined at length in the *Analects*, a collection of notes written down by Confucius's disciples after his death.

Confucius believed we can all become happy if we live our lives according to a strong moral code. His code of chivalry included living an ordered life, showing love to our family, maintaining social order, being loyal, and consciously developing our character.

Confucius pointed out that even the movement of planets follows an ordered pattern. **Therefore, to live a disordered, disorganized life goes against nature and creates disharmony.**

time alone and with others must be balanced

Some people love to be around others all the time; other people prefer to have more time to themselves. Several research studies suggest that people who spend a lot of their time alone experience higher than average rates of depression. People who live alone and introverts, for example, tend to be less happy.

However, spending all of your time with others can be unhealthy if it's used as an escape from your self. You should value your alone time as much as the time you spend with others. Everyone needs balance in these areas, so follow your instincts. **Though your head may be telling you to be alone, your heart might need company.**

alcohol is a depressant

MODERATE YOUR
alcohol CONSUMPTION

While alcohol appears to be a stimulant, it actually works as a depressant. Alcohol also plays havoc with the body's blood-sugar levels, adversely affecting our mood for several days after consumption. If that's not bad enough, regular over-consumption of alcohol slowly poisons the kidneys and impedes brain functioning.

I'm not suggesting you don't touch a drop of alcohol (in fact, several studies show a daily glass of red wine is beneficial), but I am urging you to **consume in moderation if you want to keep your mood happy and stable.**

l-tyrosine defends against depression

TAKE
L-tyrosine

L-tyrosine is an amino acid you can take to keep your mood up and your mind serene. The U.S. Army discovered that L-tyrosine was able to ward off depression and many of the effects of stress amongst the soldiers it tested.

It's easy to find sources of L-tyrosine: chicken, turkey, and most types of seafood are best. If you're vegetarian, don't worry—you can get ample amounts of L-tyrosine from tofu, beans, peas, and lentils. Or ask at your local health-food shop for an amino acid supplement that contains L-tyrosine.

Music has a high happiness success rate

If you need a boost, music can have a quick and powerful impact on your mood. In fact, playing uplifting music has an 83 percent success rate in making people feel happier.

Why not create your own happy music collection? Gather ten CDs that always make you feel good and keep them apart from the rest, ready for use when you're feeling low. **Or better still, create your own tapes or CDs of inspiring music— your personal Happiness Soundtrack.**

telling someone you care makes
both of you happier

EXPRESS YOUR
love

Telling someone how much you love them is usually going to make them feel pretty fantastic. "Being told I'm loved" ranked in the top ten most pleasant activities by subjects in a recent research study. But interestingly, it also works the other way. Wellbeing researchers P. M. Lewinsohn and M. Graf have shown that expressing our love for someone makes us feel good too. What's more, that feeling tends to stay with us throughout the day.

In the hustle and bustle of our daily lives, it's easy to forget to take the time to show our love for those we care for. Ask yourself, **"Who are the five people in the world I care about most, and when was the last time I sat down and expressed that to them?"**

meeting

new

is an uplifting part of life

MEET
new people

It's a fact that people's moods improve when they meet new people. It's easy to get into a social rut and only hang out with the same old friends. Yet weren't these great old friends once new acquaintances?

There is a strong connection between how many friends we have and how happy we tend to be. Happiness researcher Ed Diener has shown that the happiest people have both more casual and more close friends than the average person.

The truth is there are probably hundreds of people in your area who could become great pals, if only you took the time to meet them. **Join a club, take up a hobby, or attend a new social event each week.** Creating regular opportunities to meet new people isn't just fun—it will inevitably lead to new lifelong friends.

watching tv can bring you down

TURN off THE TV

Here's a weird fact: the average person now watches over four hours of television each day, yet research clearly shows it doesn't make us feel any better. **In fact, the most common reported emotion while watching the box is mild depression.**

It gets worse. A recent study showed that watching a lot of TV vastly increases our craving for more possessions, and every hour we watch reduces our contentment by around 5 percent.

It's time we turned off the box. First, make a pact with your family to have the TV on only three nights a week. Then work on reducing your viewing time even further over the next six months.

feeling sexy has excellent mental benefits

DRESS sexily

A study by wellbeing researchers P. M. Lewinsohn and M. Graf showed that being perceived as sexually attractive by another person considerably enhances our mood. **And what's more, we feel more positive for the whole day.**

So don't leave it to chance. **When appropriate, take the time to make yourself look good—even sexy—and you'll enjoy the mental benefits.** Just wearing something especially flattering or putting in an extra effort when getting ready in the morning can be a huge confidence boost. By the way, that study also highlighted the importance of telling someone else when you find them attractive (under appropriate circumstances, of course!).

you can't go past a pet

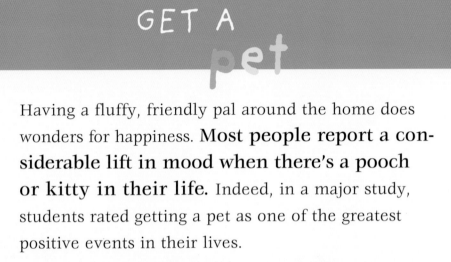

GET A pet

Having a fluffy, friendly pal around the home does wonders for happiness. **Most people report a considerable lift in mood when there's a pooch or kitty in their life.** Indeed, in a major study, students rated getting a pet as one of the greatest positive events in their lives.

Your landlord won't allow a pet? No problem. Go down to the park in the mornings and give other people's pets a pat. It's almost impossible not to be uplifted when you give affection to animals, whether they're yours or someone else's.

sharing activities leads to shared happiness

CREATE AN activity group

As we've seen, almost every activity is enjoyed more with friends. So, why not organize a weekly activity group to make social leisure activities more regular? In his brilliant book *The Psychology of Happiness,* Michael Argyle shows how much activity groups can enhance the wellbeing of everyone involved.

Here's how it might work: **Put together a list of five or six people you enjoy being with and whom you feel would get along with each other.** Introduce the concept of the activity group and get each person to commit to coming up with one novel activity every month or so. That way, you'll have at least one enjoyable event to look forward to every week. Over a year, that adds up to closer friendships, many new experiences, and a huge increase in fun.

kissing just feels great

kiss SOMEONE

We all like a good smooch. Maybe because a kiss is a form of affectionate interaction with another person, maybe because we like how it feels, maybe simply because it indicates that someone really likes us. (In some cases, really, *really* likes us!) Whatever the reason, science backs up what most of us intuitively feel—that **kissing makes us feel happier.**

So, are you kissing enough? Could you arrange more kissing moments with your partner? Or if you're single, could you figure our more ways to get some more lip smacking in your life? However you manage it, **remember that kissing may be a simple thing— but it can have a truly wonderful effect on your smile-o-meter.**

study happiness every day

FOCUS ON happiness

Perhaps the most important technique I have saved until last. If you genuinely want to have a high level of happiness in your life, it is crucial that you **focus on your happiness every day.** You must decide to be happy now, not some time in the future.

Happiness cannot be left on the backburner for when you have some spare time or when you're feeling down. Happiness is both an art and a science, and it deserves regular study and fine-tuning.

You now have access to numerous techniques that have been proven to increase your levels of joy and wellbeing. Use them. Become an expert at applying them. Make them a part of you. If you do, a happier life is yours.

recommended reading

Baker, Dan, and Cameron Stauth, *What Happy People Know* (New York: St. Martin's Griffin, 2004).

Beck, Martha, *The Joy Diet* (New York: Crown, 2003).

Benson, Herbert, *The Relaxation Response* (New York: HarperCollins, 2000).

Csikszentmihalyi, Mihaly, *Flow: The Psychology of Optimal Experience* (New York: HarperCollins, 1990).

The Dalai Lama, and Harold Cutler, *The Art of Happiness* (New York: Riverhead Books, 1998).

Dwoskin, Hale, and Jack Canfield, *The Sedona Method* (Sedona, AZ: Sedona Press, 2003).

Myers, David, *The Pursuit of Happiness* (New York: Perrenial Currents, 1993).

Niven, David, *The 100 Simple Secrets of Happy People* (San Francisco: HarperSanFrancisco, 2000).

Null, Gary, *The Food-Mood-Body Connection* (New York: Seven Stories Press, 2000).

Seligman, Martin, *Authentic Happiness* (New York: Free Press, 2004).

Thayer, Robert E., *Calm Energy* (New York: Oxford University Press, 2003).

about the author

siimon reynolds is one of the most well-known and respected names in advertising. He has won almost every major advertising award for creativity in the world, including the Gold Lion at Cannes, the Gold Pencil at the New York One Show, and the Grand Prize at the London International Advertising Festival. In Australia, he has won Newspaper Ad of the Year, TV Commercial of the Year, Magazine Ad of the Year, and Advertising Agency of the Year (twice).

Siimon is a winner of the International Advertising Association Scholarship and NSW Young Career Achiever of the Year. He has lectured nationally on advertising to over 50,000 businesspeople, and is a successful author in six countries. He is now Creative Director of Love, an advertising, public relations, and brand-building company, and cofounder of the Photon Group, a consortium of thirteen marketing companies, which recently listed on the Australian Stock Exchange.